PRESIDENTIAL TRANSITIONS
1960-2001

PRESIDENTIAL TRANSITIONS 1960-2001

STEPHANIE SMITH

Novinka Books
New York

Senior Editors: Susan Boriotti and Donna Dennis
Coordinating Editor: Tatiana Shohov
Office Manager: Annette Hellinger
Graphics: Wanda Serrano
Editorial Production: Vladimir Klestov, Matthew Kozlowski and Maya Columbus
Circulation: Ave Maria Gonzalez, Vera Popovic, Luis Aviles, Raymond Davis, Melissa Diaz and Jeannie Pappas
Communications and Acquisitions: Serge P. Shohov
Marketing: Cathy DeGregory

Library of Congress Cataloging-in-Publication Data

ISBN: 1-59033-511-2

Copyright © 2003 by Novinka Books, An Imprint of
Nova Science Publishers, Inc.
400 Oser Ave, Suite 1600
Hauppauge, New York 11788-3619
Tele. 631-231-7269   Fax 631-231-8175
e-mail: Novascience@earthlink.net
Web Site: http://www.novapublishers.com

All rights reserved. No part of this book may be reproduced, stored in a retrieval system or transmitted in any form or by any means: electronic, electrostatic, magnetic, tape, mechanical photocopying, recording or otherwise without permission from the publishers.

The authors and publisher have taken care in preparation of this book, but make no expressed or implied warranty of any kind and assume no responsibility for any errors or omissions. No liability is assumed for incidental or consequential damages in connection with or arising out of information contained in this book.

This publication is designed to provide accurate and authoritative information with regard to the subject matter covered herein. It is sold with the clear understanding that the publisher is not engaged in rendering legal or any other professional services. If legal or any other expert assistance is required, the services of a competent person should be sought. FROM A DECLARATION OF PARTICIPANTS JOINTLY ADOPTED BY A COMMITTEE OF THE AMERICAN BAR ASSOCIATION AND A COMMITTEE OF PUBLISHERS.

Printed in the United States of America

CONTENTS

Summary vii

PART 1:	PRESIDENTIAL TRANSITIONS	1
Chapter 1	Introduction	3
Chapter 2	President's Commission on Campaign Costs	5
	The Presidential Transition Act of 1963	6
	Funding Under the Presidential Transition Act	7
	Presidential Transitions Effectiveness Act	10
	Funding Under the Presidential Transitions Effectiveness Act	12
	Presidential Transition Act of 2000	13
	Online Resources	14
	Activities of Past Presidential Transitions	15
	Eisenhower-Kennedy Transition	15
	Johnson-Nixon Transition	17
	Nixon-Ford Transition	18
	Ford-Carter Transition	19
	Carter-Reagan Transition	20
	Reagan-Bush Transition	22
	Bush-Clinton Transition	23
	General Considerations	24
	Organizational Decisions	26
	Continuity of the Federal Government	27
	Setting Priorities in the New Administration	28

PART 2:	TEXT OF PRESIDENTIAL TRANSITION STATUTES	**29**
Chapter 3	Presidential Transition Act of 2000: P.L. 106-293, October 13, 2000	**31**
	An Act	31
Chapter 4	Presidential Transitions Effectiveness Act: P.L. 100-398, August 17, 1988; 102 Stat. 985	**35**
	An Act	35
Chapter 5	Presidential Transition Act of 1963, Amendments: P.L. 94-499, October 14, 1976; 90 Stat. 2380	**43**
	An Act	43
Chapter 6	Presidential Transition Act of 1963: P.L. 88-277, March 7, 1964; 78 Stat. 153	**45**
	An Act	45
Index		**51**

SUMMARY

On Inauguration Day, January 20, 2001, when the newly-elected President takes the oath of office, the nation will undergo its first formal transfer of presidential power since 1993. Aside from this symbolic transfer of power, an orderly transition from the outgoing Administration to the incoming Administration is essential to ensure continuity in the working affairs of government. Necessary funding for both the incoming and outgoing Administrations is authorized by the Presidential Transition Act, as amended. The General Services Administration (GSA) is authorized to provide suitable office space, staff compensation, communications services, and printing and postage costs associated with the transition. For FY2001, GSA is authorized a total of $7.1 million for the upcoming transition: $1.83 million for the outgoing Clinton Administration; $4.27 million for the incoming Administration; and $1 million for GSA to provide additional assistance as required by the recently-enacted Presidential Transition Act of 2000.

Part I of this book discusses legislative actions to enhance the transition process, each transition since 1960, and general considerations for the presidential transition process. Part II contains the text of the major transition statutes.

Part 1: Presidential Transitions

Chapter 1

INTRODUCTION

Since outgoing President George Washington first relinquished his office to incoming President John Adams in 1797, this peaceful transition, symbolizing both continuity and change, has demonstrated the "best of American democracy to the world."[1] In reality, however, the activities surrounding a presidential transition today begin shortly after the election, as the President-elect has fewer than 11 weeks to formulate the new administration before taking the oath of office on January 20. A formal transition process has been shown to be essential to ensure continuity in the conduct of the affairs of the executive branch, as well as the rest of the federal government.

Before 1963, the primary source of funding for transition expenses was the political party organization of the incoming President and the efforts of volunteer staff. Realizing the importance of presidential transitions for effective government, Congress first enacted the Presidential Transition Act of 1963 (PTA) to authorize federal funding and assistance for future incoming Administrations.[2] The Act was amended by Congress in 1976, to increase the authorization for a presidential transition to $3 million, with $2 million available to the President-elect and Vice President-elect and $1 million to the outgoing President and Vice President.[3]

---

[1] Alvin S. Felzenberg, ed., *The Keys to a Successful Presidency* (Washington: Heritage Foundation, 2000), p. 7. For a detailed discussion of early presidential transitions, see also: Laurin L. Henry, *Presidential Transitions* (Washington: Brookings Institution, 1960). A discussion of the four most recent transitions can be found in: John P. Burke, *Presidential Transitions: From Politics to Practice* (Colorado: Lynne Rienner Publishers, 2000).

[2] P.L. 88-277, March 4, 1964; 78 Stat. 153; 3 U.S.C. 102 note. Although signed in 1964, the Act carries the 1963 designation 002E

[3] P. L. 94-499, Oct. 14, 1976; 90 Stat. 2380.

In 1988, Congress enacted the Presidential Transitions Effectiveness Act to increase federal funding to $5 million to support a change of Administrations.[4] Of this total, $3.5 million was authorized to be appropriated for services and facilities to the President-elect and Vice President-elect. The outgoing President and Vice President were authorized $1.5 million in federal funds. A total of $250,000 would be returned to the Treasury if the outgoing Vice President were subsequently elected President. These funds were authorized to be increased in future transitions to accommodate inflation. The new legislation also amended the PTA to require that private contributions and names of transition personnel be publicly disclosed.

In anticipation of the 2000-2001 transition, the 106th Congress recently enacted P.L. 106-293, the Presidential Transition Act of 2000, which President Clinton signed on October 13, 2000.[5] It amends the PTA to authorize the General Services Administration (GSA) to provide additional support in the orientation of the President-elect's newly-appointed senior staff.

Part I of this book discusses legislative actions to enhance the transition process, each transition since the 1960-1961 arrival of President John F. Kennedy, and general considerations for the presidential transition process. Part II contains the text of the major transition statutes discussed in the book.

---

[4] P.L. 100-398, Aug. 17, 1988; 102 Stat. 985.
[5] P.L. 106-293, Oct. 13, 2000.

Chapter 2

PRESIDENT'S COMMISSION ON CAMPAIGN COSTS

Subsequent to the 1960 election, it was widely recognized that changes were needed in campaign finance practices. Funding for presidential transition activities was among the issues discussed. Accordingly, on November 8, 1961, President Kennedy established the President's Commission on Campaign Costs to make recommendations on "improved ways of financing expenditures required of nominees for the offices of President and Vice President" as well as other relevant costs associated with presidential campaigns.[1] Five months later, the 12-member bipartisan commission completed its final report, entitled *Financing Presidential Campaigns,* which included a recommendation on presidential transitions.[2]

The commission reported that the 1952-1953 transition for President Dwight D. Eisenhower cost a special Republican committee more than $200,000, and the 1960-1961 transition for President Kennedy cost $360,000, funded by the Democratic National Committee. Noting that such expenses created financial hardship for the political parties, especially after an election, the commission recommended that funding for the President-elect and Vice President-elect should not be the responsibility of a political party.

> We endorse proposals to "institutionalize" the transition from one administration to another when the party in power changes. Important

---

[1] Establishing the President's Commission on Campaign Costs, E.O. 10974, Nov. 8, 1961, 3 CFR 496 (1959-1963 Compilation).
[2] U.S. President's Commission on Campaign Costs, *Financing Presidential Campaigns,* Apr. 1962 (Washington: GPO, 1962), p. 36.

reasons for doing so exist wholly aside from the costs to the parties. The new President must select and assemble the staff to man his administration, and they in return must prepare themselves for their new responsibilities.[3]

The commission also recommended that the outgoing President be authorized to receive federally-funded facilities and services to assist in the orderly transfer of executive power.[4]

In a May 29, 1962 letter to Congress transmitting legislation to implement the commission's final recommendations, President Kennedy stated:

> Traditionally, the political parties have had to par the costs of the President-elect and Vice President-elect during the transition period between the election and the inauguration of a new Administration. It is entirely desirable and appropriate that the Federal government provide funds for paying the reasonable and necessary costs of installing a new Administration in office.[5]

In addition to the importance of federal funding, President Kennedy stressed that an incoming President must select "responsible public officials who must prepare themselves for their new responsibilities" during the transition period.

THE PRESIDENTIAL TRANSITION ACT OF 1963

As recommended by the President's Commission on Campaign Costs, legislation was introduced during the 87th Congress to provide federal financial support for presidential transitions. Although it was supported by President Kennedy, there was no action on the bill. During the following Congress, H.R. 4638, the Presidential Transition Act of 1963 (PTA), was introduced on April 24, 1963 and was enacted on March 7, 1964 as Public Law 88-277.[6]

The PTA authorized the Administrator of General Services to provide to the President-elect and Vice President-elect office space, compensation to

---

[3] Ibid., pp. 23-24.
[4] Ibid., p. 24.
[5] President John F. Kennedy, 1962, Public Papers of the Presidents, Letter to the President o[the Senate and to the Speaker of the House Transmitting Bills to Garry Out Recommendations of the Commission on Campaign Costs, May 29, 1962 (Washington: GPO, 1963), p. 446.
[6] 3 U.S.C. 102 note.

office staff, the detail of personnel on a reimbursable or non-reimbursable basis from federal agencies, the hiring of consultants, and travel expenses. It also authorized the provision of such services to the outgoing President and Vice President, for a period not to exceed six months from the expiration of their terms of office. The act authorized the appropriation of $900,000 for each presidential transition, but did not specify how the amount was to be divided between the incoming and outgoing Administrations. However, the legislative history indicated that the funds were to be divided equally.[7]

FUNDING UNDER THE PRESIDENTIAL TRANSITION ACT

Even though the PTA was enacted in 1964, its provisions were not fully applied following President Johnson's reelection in 1964, since he was already in office. Vice President-elect Hubert Humphrey spent approximately $72,000 in transition expenses under the Act.[8]

Johnson-Nixon Transition

The PTA was first fully implemented during the transition from the Administration of President Johnson to that of President Richard Nixon in 1968-1969, when the transition funds were divided equally between the two Administrations. The following year, the General Accounting Office (GAO) reviewed the operation of the Act. GAO found that President Nixon incurred transition costs of $1.5 million, and it recommended that the $900,000 limit be increased to better reflect actual transition expenses.[9] A 1982 GAO report stated that President-elect Nixon raised $1 million in private funds to supplement the $450,000 available to him under the Act.[10]

President Johnson spent $370,276 of the $375,000 allocated to him under the PTA.[11] He also had the assistance of employees provided by

---

[7] V.S. Congress, Senate Committee on Government Operations, *Presidential Transition Act, Distribution of Federal Surplus Property, and Records Management,* hearings, 94th Cong., 2nd sess., Sept. 13, 1976 (Washington: GPO, 1976), p. 3.
[8] V.S. General Accounting Office, *Federal Assistance for Presidential Transitions,* Nov. 16, 1970 (Washington: GPO, 1970), p. 24.
[9] Ibid., p. 3.
[10] U.S. General Accounting Office, *The Reagan-Bush Transition Team's Activities at Six Selected Agencies,* Jan. 28, 1982 (Washington: GPO, 1982), p. 3.
[11] GAO, Federal Assistance for Presidential Transitions, pp. 41-42.

federal agencies on a nonreimbursable basis.[12] Vice President Humphrey spent $75,000 to pay the salaries and expenses of his staff and consultants.[13]

Nixon-Ford Transition

In 1974, Vice President Gerald Ford faced a situation entirely different from that of the first presidential transition covered by the PTA. Because of the resignation of President Nixon, Mr. Ford was not a President-elect, and he received no funds under the Presidential Transition Act.[14]

Due to the manner in which President Nixon left, office, there was some debate as to whether he was entitled to allowances and services as a former President. The Justice Department ruled that he was entitled to federal funds as a former President, since he had not been removed by impeachment.[15] Funds are appropriated under the Presidential Transition Act only for presidential election years; therefore, no funds were specifically available when President Nixon left office. On August 29, 1974, the Ford Administration requested Congress to appropriate $450,000 to GSA for carrying out the provisions of the Act. The Supplemental Appropriations Act of 1975 appropriated $100,000 to President Nixon under the Presidential Transition Act for a period of six months ending February 9, 1975.[16] In addition, most of the clerical and staff work was clone by detailed employees provided by several federal agencies, on a nonreimbursable basis.[17]

Ford-Carter Transition

Based on earlier GAO recommendations, the Presidential Transition Act was amended by Congress in 1976, to increase the authorization for a presidential transition to $3 million, with $2 million available to the President-elect and Vice President-elect and $1 million to the outgoing

---

[12] V.S. General Accounting Office, *Audit of Ford-Carter Presidential Transition Expenditures,* Dec. 23, 1977 (Washington: GPO, 1977), p. i.

[13] GAO, Federal Assistance for Presidential Transitions, p. 45.

[14] U.S. General Accounting Office, *Recommendations for Changes in Legislation,* Dec. 24, 1975 (Washington: GPO, 1975), p. 2.

[15] V.S. Department of Justice, Office of Assistant Attorney General, letter to the Administrator of the General Services Administration from Mary C. Lawton, Acting Assistant Attorney General, Office of Legal Counsel, Washington, DC, Aug. 15, 1974.

[16] P .L. 93-554, Dec. 27, 1974; 88 Stat. 1771, at 1782. An additional amount of $100,000 was also appropriated to former President Nixon for pension, allowances, and office staff under the Former Presidents Act (3 U.S.C. 102 note).

[17] GAO, Recommendations for Changes in Legislation, pp. 5-6.

President and Vice President.[18] The Act also amended the earlier legislation to authorize the detail of personnel, on a reimbursable basis only.

The increase in funding was first made available to President Ford and President Jimmy Carter in the 1976-1977 transition. The incoming Carter-Mondale Administration spent approximately $1.7 million of the $2 million made available to it pursuant to the Act, without any reported private additional assistance.[19]

Of the $1 million appropriated to the outgoing Ford Administration, President Ford was allocated $905,000, and $95,000 went to Vice President Nelson "Rockefeller. As of August 31, 1977, former President Ford had spent approximately, $635,000 of the total appropriation, but GAO found that an additional amount would be needed to pay for the use of military aircraft.[20]

At the end of the six-month transition period, Vice President Rockefeller had used $51,292 of the total funds available to him under the PTA, as amended.[21]

Carter-Reagan Transition

During the 1980-1981 transition, President Carter spent $672,659 for transition purposes, and Vice President Walter Mondale used $188,867 of the $1 million available to the outgoing Carter Administration.[22]

The incoming Administration of Ronald Reagan spent approximately $1.75 million of the $2 million in available transition funds. Of this total, $63,378, went to Vice President-elect George H. W. Bush for personnel compensation and benefits.[23]

A 1982 GAO review of the Reagan-Bush transition team's activities at six federal agencies found that approximately $235,000 in transition-related expenses were charged to the agencies' general appropriations. According to GAO, the most of the expenses were incurred for gathering and communicating information about agency operations to the transition team. However, certain expenses were related to salaries for secretarial employees who were assigned to the transition team on a nonreimbursable basis and who worked at the team's direction on a full-time or nearly full-time basis.

---

[18] P.L. 94-499, Oct. 14, 1976; 90 Stat. 2380; 3 U.S.C. 102 note.
[19] GAO, The Reagan-Bush Transition Team's Activities at Six Selected Agencies, p. 3.
[20] GAO, Audit of Ford-Carter Presidential Transition Expenditures, p. n.
[21] Ibid., pp. 11-12.
[22] Data obtained from General Services Administration, Nov. 28, 1990.
[23] Ibid.

Since the PTA authorized that agency employee details to the transition team be made on a reimbursable basis only, GAO found that the transition team did not always follow correct procedures.[24]

In addition to federal appropriations, funds for the Reagan transition were solicited from the public by the Presidential Transition Foundation, Inc., a private corporation. GAO attempted to audit these funds, but was denied access to the accounts and records by the foundation's legal counsel. According to GAO's report, the foundation stated that a public accounting firm would audit it. GAO found that federal funds appropriated under the PTA were kept separate from private funds donated to the foundation.[25] A 1988 Senate report stated that, based on Internal Revenue Service documents and Federal Election Commission reports:

> ... President-elect Reagan raised approximately $1.25 million for both his Pre-election and post-election transition activities in 1980. None of the sources or expenditures associated with the private cash were ever disclosed to the public, creating the potential for hidden conflicts of interest.[26]

PRESIDENTIAL TRANSITIONS EFFECTIVENESS ACT

In anticipation of a new President being elected in the November 1988 general election, the 100th Congress began consideration of legislation to provide increased federal funding for the 1988-1989 transition. After examining the transition expenditures for previous incoming Presidents Carter and Reagan, the Senate Committee on Governmental Affairs expressed concern that future incoming Presidents would have to raise private funds to finance their transitions if the funding under the PTA were not increased.[27]

Prior to the enactment of the PTA, and subsequently, many candidates had initiated transition activities and studies before the election, in some cases before the convention. The committee affirmed that pre-election transition planning is a legitimate cost of a presidential transition and concluded that such planning should be covered, at least partially, by public

---

[24] OAO, Reagan-Bush Transition Team's Activities at Six: Selected Agencies, p. iv.
[25] U.S. General Accounting Office, *Audit of Reagan Presidential Transition Expenditures*, March 2, 1981 (Washington: GPO, 1981), p. 1.
[26] U.S. Congress, Senate, *Presidential Transitions Effectiveness Act of* 1988, April 20, 1988, S. Rept. 100-317, 100th Cong., 2nd sess. (Washington: OPO, 1988), p. 10.
[27] Ibid., pp. 4-5.

funds. However, the Federal Elections Commission indicated that there were regulatory prohibitions:

> ... it appears that, under current law and regulations, the FEC would find that federal campaign funds-as opposed to segregated private donations-are not available for transition funding during a campaign. Furthermore, we are aware of no FEC reporting or disclosure requirements applicable to private transition funds.[28]

As reported, the Senate bill provided for limited public funding of pre-election transition planning. Those provisions were not enacted. It continues to be the practice that all pre-election transition planning is privately financed.

As a result of these deliberations, Congress enacted the Presidential Transitions Effectiveness Act to increase federal funding for presidential transitions and to amend the 1964 legislation to require that private contributions and names of transition personnel be publicly disclosed (see Part II for complete text).[29]

The act authorized $3.5 million to be appropriated for the funding of services and facilities to the President-elect and Vice President-elect. The outgoing President and Vice President were authorized $1.5 million in federal funds. In the event the outgoing Vice President were subsequently elected President, the new Administration would receive only $1.25 million in assistance. For future transitions, these figures were to be increased by an inflation-adjusted amount, based on actual costs of transition expenses and services of the most recent presidential transition.

In addition to funding provisions, the new legislation amended the PTA to require that private contributions and names of transition personnel be publicly disclosed. As a condition for receiving federal funding and services, the President-elect and Vice President-elect must formally disclose the date, source, and amount of all privately-contributed funds for the transition, with a maximum contribution of $5,000 allowed from any person or organization. These written disclosures must be made to GSA within 30 days after the January 20 inauguration. The President-elect must also disclose information about transition team members before initial contact with a federal department or agency. The Act also limits any temporary appointment to an executive branch vacancy to 120 days, unless a nomination has been submitted to the Senate.

---

[28] Ibid., p. 7
[29] P.L. 100-398, Aug. 17, 1988, 102 Stat. 985.

FUNDING UNDER THE PRESIDENTIAL TRANSITIONS EFFECTIVENESS ACT

As authorized by the Act, the funding for an incoming Administration is available from the day following the general elections until 30 days after the inauguration. For the outgoing President and Vice President, transition funding was extended from six to seven months, beginning one month before the inauguration, to facilitate their relocation to private life. Separate legislation also provides former Presidents an annual lifetime pension and staff and office allowances after the transition period expires, as well as Secret Service protection.[30]

The increase in funding under the Presidential Transitions Effectiveness Act was first made available during the 1988-1989 transition of outgoing President Reagan and his successor, George Bush.

President Reagan used $697,034 of the $1.25 million available to him under the Act as the outgoing President.[31] Outgoing Vice President Bush was authorized $250,000 for expenses related to his transition from that office. The $250,000 was transferred to the Federal Election Commission.[32] Incoming President Bush and Vice President Dan Quayle spent $2.3 million of the $3.5 million authorized under the PTA, as amended, and transferred $1 million to the Government of the District of Columbia for inaugural expenses.[33]

For the 1992-1993 presidential transition, $3.5 million was appropriated to GSA for the incoming Administration of President Clinton and Vice President Albert Gore Jr., and $1.5 million for the outgoing Administration of President Bush and Vice President Quayle.[34] Of this total, the Bush Administration determined that $1.2 million would be made available to President Bush, with the remaining $250,000 to be used by Vice President Quayle. During his transition period, President Bush used $907,939, with an unobligated balance of $342,061. Vice President Quayle used $244,192 for

---

[30] See: V.S. Library of Congress, Congressional Research Service, *Former Presidents: Federal Pension and Retirement Benefits*, by Stephanie Smith, CRS Report 98-249 GOV (Washington: June 26, 2000).
[31] Data supplied by General Services Administration, Nov. 28, 1990.
[32] Dire Emergency Supplemental Appropriations and Transfers, Urgent Supplementals, and Correcting Enrollment Errors Act of 1989, P..L. 101-45, June 30, 1989; 103 Stat. 126.
[33] P.L. 101-45, June 30, 1989; 103 Stat. 116; see also: U.S. Congress, House, Committee on Appropriations, Subcommittee on the Treasury, Postal Service, and General Government Appropriations, *Treasury, Postal Service, and General Government Appropriations for Fiscal Year* 1993, part 5, Feb. 25, 1992, hearings (Washington: OPO, 1992), p. 536.
[34] P.L. 102-393, Oct. 5, 1992; 106 Stat. 1729.

transition expenses, with an unobligated balance of $5,808. President Clinton and Vice President Gore jointly spent $3,485,000, with an unobligated balance of $15,000. For FY1997, $5.6 million was authorized in the event of a presidential transition in January 1997, which did not occur.[35]

For FY2001, GSA requested a total of $7.1 million for the upcoming presidential transition. Of this total, $1.83 million is budgeted for the outgoing Clinton Administration, with $305,000 to be returned to the Treasury if Vice President Albert Gore is elected President; $4.27 million is requested for the incoming Administration. GSA requested an additional $1 million to fund its new responsibilities under the Presidential Transition Act of 2000. On October 12, 2000, the Senate gave final approval to the conference agreement that would have funded this account at $7.1 million in the FY2001 Treasury, Postal Service, and General Government Appropriations Act.[36] On October 30, President Clinton vetoed the legislation. On November 3, 2000, President Clinton signed the measure that funds the 2000-2001 transition at the requested levels.[37]

PRESIDENTIAL TRANSITION ACT OF 2000

While the PTA, as amended, has authorized federal funds and facilities to ensure smooth transitions in the past, no formalized attention was given to orientation of a President-elect's newly-appointed senior staff. In anticipation of the upcoming 2000-2001 transition, the 106th Congress enacted P.L. 106-293, the Presidential Transition Act of 2000, which President Clinton signed on October 13, 2000. It amends the PTA to authorize GSA to provide additional support during the upcoming 2000-2001 transition period. Most importantly, GSA will coordinate the development and presentation of orientation sessions for the President-elect's nominees for cabinet and high-level executive branch positions. Prior to the election on November 7, GSA was authorized to consult with presidential candidates in order to begin development of a computer and communications system for use during the transition period. In conjunction with the National Archives and Records Administration (NARA), GSA is also required to create a transition directory, composed of federal publications and materials pertaining to the statutory and administrative functions of each federal department and agency. A fourth major provision

---

[35] Data provided by GSA Budget Office in Oct. 23, 2000 telephone conversation.
[36] H.R. 4516, section 1001, Title IV; vetoed Oct. 30, 2000.
[37] P.L.106-426, Nov. 3, 2000.

requires the Office of Government Ethics to prepare a report on needed improvements to the financial disclosure process currently required for presidential nominees.

Passage of the Presidential Transition Act of 2000 was intended to allow the President-elect and his appointees to "hit the ground running" as they take office on January 20, and increase their effectiveness during the crucial first year in office. In mid-November, it was still unclear whether the inauguration summarizing the outcome of the 2000 presidential election would have a significant impact on the transition. According to presidential scholar Dwight Ink, key provisions of the new legislation pertaining to a formal orientation process between political appointees and career federal employees could lead to better working relationships during the next tour years.[38]

ONLINE RESOURCES

In order to facilitate the 2000-2001 presidential transition process, several online web sites have been created:

- The Office of Personnel Management (OPM) maintains an online transition employment guide pertaining to departing employees, newly appointed employees, and the career service [http://www.opm.gov/transition/index.htm].
- The Brookings Institution has established the "Presidential Appointee Initiative," funded by a grant from the Pew Charitable Trusts, to assist newly-appointed officials during the transition period [http://www.appointee.brookings.org].
- The Senate Committee on Governmental Affairs provides a range of transition issues and policies [http://www.senate.gov/~gov_affairs/transitions/pta_index.htm].
- The Council for Excellence in Government provides online transcripts of former government officials discussing the transition candidates must make from campaigning to governing [http://www.excelgov.org/]

Additional sites will be available as the transition period begins.

---

[38] Jennifer Miller, "New Legislation Will Impact Presidential Transitions," *PA Times*, Feb. 2000, p. 1.

ACTIVITIES OF PAST PRESIDENTIAL TRANSITIONS

Before the Eisenhower/Kennedy transition in 1961-1962 and the subsequent enactment of the Presidential Transition Act of 1963, communications between incoming and outgoing Administrations were usually limited, especially when the President and President-elect were of different political parties and had been recent campaign opponents. It was generally expected that the President-elect would remain away from Washington until Inauguration Day. Formal communications were conducted concerning the inaugural ceremonies and the occupancy of the White House, but with virtually no discussion of substantive issues. The new cabinet of the incoming Administration was generally not selected until shortly before Inauguration Day; therefore, meetings between incoming and outgoing cabinet members were not common.[39]

President Harry Truman, who had been thrust into the Presidency in 1945 following President Franklin D. Roosevelt's sudden death, helped to establish the tradition that an outgoing President should actively facilitate the transition of power to an incoming President. Following the election on November 5, 1952, President Truman sent a telegram to President-elect Dwight D. Eisenhower, inviting him to a meeting in the White House "to discuss the problems of this transition period, so that it may be made clear to all the world that this Nation is united in its struggle for freedom and peace".[40] President Truman also required each of the executive branch agencies to report to him on what was being done to facilitate the transition.[41]

In spite of the serious responsibilities involved, only within the past 30 years, since the enactment of the PTA have the problems associated with the transition of power received much systematic attention.

EISENHOWER-KENNEDY TRANSITION

Following his election in 1960, President Kennedy entered the White House well-briefed for his assumption of responsibility. While still a

---

[39] Laurin L. Henry, *Presidential Transitions* (Washington: The Brookings Institution, 1960), p. 58. This book provides an in-depth study of presidential transitions before 1960.
[40] President Harry S. Truman, 1952-1953, Public Papers of the Presidents, *Letter of invitation to the President-Elect,* Nov. 6, 1952 (Washington: GPO, 1953), pp. 1048-1049.
[41] Hemy, Pesidential Transitions, pp. 513-514.

candidate, Senator Kennedy commissioned various documents on the transition process and post-election issues.[42]

Numerous authors and historians credit President-elect Kennedy's preparation for transition to office in 1960-1961 as being unprecedented in the history of presidential transitions. A 1960 review of past presidential transitions by the *Congressional Quarterly* reported that:

> John F. Kennedy made an important innovation in American Presidential transitions through his appointment of 29 task forces which were asked to report to him on a wide variety of domestic and foreign policy problems in the period immediately preceding and following his inauguration.
>
> ... While other Presidents-elect sometimes asked individual political associates or small groups of experts to brief them on limited phases of public policy, there is no precedent for the large number of task forces, some with wide memberships, which submitted detailed policy briefings to Kennedy near the time of his inauguration.[43]

Senator Kennedy's use of task forces began soon after his July 1960 Democratic presidential nomination, when he recognized that, if elected President, he would need policy-making advice to address the critical issues that would face him immediately upon taking office. Senator Kennedy asked two of his former opponents for the Democratic presidential nomination, Governor Adlai Stevenson and Senator Stuart Symington, to head the first two task forces on foreign policy and national defense issues. Senator Kennedy, before election day, appointed five additional task forces pertaining to foreign affairs, natural resources, domestic agriculture, and the overseas food program. The creation of these task forces served to highlight his interest in diverse issues, while at the same time using the expertise of former political opponents to demonstrate their support of Senator Kennedy's candidacy.[44]

All of the taskforce members were volunteers who received no compensation. One task force project was funded by a foundation grant of $20,000. As stated earlier, the Democratic National Committee paid $350,000 of Kennedy's administrative expenses for the transition.[45]

Immediately following the election, President-elect Kennedy, with the assistance of Theodore Sorensen as counsel-designate to the President, made

---

[42] David T. Stanley, *Changing Administrations* (Washington: Brookings Institution, 1965), p.6.
[43] "Pre-Inaugural Task Forces Unprecedented in History ," *Congressional Quarterly Weekly Report,* vol. 19, April 7, 1961, p. 620.
[44] Ibid.
[45] Ibid., p. 621.

a detailed listing of which task forces to appoint, with a deadline for submission of a final report. By his inauguration, President Kennedy had appointed 29 task forces, equally divided between foreign and domestic policy. Of this total, 24 task forces had already submitted final reports that contained precise recommendations. According to the *Congressional Quarterly,* approximately one person from each task force was to be appointed to a high level position within the new Administration.[46]

Washington, D.C. attorney Clark Clifford was appointed to be in charge of transition period relations with the outgoing Eisenhower Administration. When notified of an upcoming January 6, 1961 meeting between President-elect Kennedy and President Eisenhower, Mr. Clifford was able to present an extensive background briefing and report to Mr. Kennedy based on the task force position papers.[47]

JOHNSON-NIXON TRANSITION

It was during the 1968-1969 transition that the Presidential Transition Act was first used for both incoming and outgoing Administrations. As an incumbent President not running for re-election, President Johnson became the first President to invite the presidential candidates and their staff to plan for the transition before the November election.[48]

Richard M. Nixon 'began planning for an efficient transition following his nomination at the Republican National Convention in July 1968. Franklin Lincoln, Jr., an attorney and former Defense Department official, was appointed as Mr. Nixon's representative on transition matters. Mr. Nixon made use of reports of past presidential transition efforts, and made lists of early decisions that would need to be made if he were elected to office. Following his November 1968 election, President-elect Nixon created approximately 30 task forces to prepare recommendations on issues pertaining to housing, education, tax policy, transportation, foreign aid, and job training.[49]

By the end of November 1968, President-elect Nixon had selected his first high level appointees who would be responsible for implementing policies for his Administration. In December 1968, he met with Republican

---

[46] Ibid.
[47] Ibid.
[48] "Presidential Transition," *Congressional Quarterly Weekly Report,* Sept. 20, 1968, val. 26, p. 2506.
[49] Alan L. Otten, "Nixon Works to Ensure an Efficient Take-Over If He Gains Presidency," *Wall Street Journal,* Oct. 25, 1968, p. 1.

leaders to discuss his future legislative agenda. The selection of the Nixon cabinet was a long process, in which the President-elect spent six weeks studying various alternatives.[50]

NIXON-FORD TRANSITION

The unprecedented series of events culminating in President Nixon's resignation from office complicated the process of transition for Vice President Ford in 1974. Transition plans were initiated by Vice President Ford's close friend and former law partner Philip Buchen, who had concluded that events might force an untimely end to the Nixon Administration. According to published sources, Mr. Buchen conducted several meetings to discuss details for the change of Administrations in the event of resignation or impeachment. Assisting in the transition planning were Nixon adviser Clay Whitehead, Governor William Scranton, Senator Robert Griffin, Representative John Byrnes, former Nixon aide Bryce Harlow, and William Whyte of U.S. Steel.

One day before his formal resignation announcement to the public on August 9, 1974, President Nixon informed Vice President Ford of his intention to resign. The same day, Mr. Ford's transition planners began preparing formal documents with policy alternatives that President Ford would have to consider immediately upon taking office. The morning of Mr. Ford's swearing-in as President, advisers met at the Ford residence to brief him on their transition documents.[51]

Upon assuming the presidency, President Ford asked all members of former President Nixon's cabinet and the heads of all federal agencies to remain in his Administration for continuity and stability.[52] By December 1974, the cabinet members and numerous high-ranking aides submitted their resignations to the President. During this period, President Ford came under criticism for the allegedly slow pace at which he had replaced Nixon appointees and selected their successors. In response, Mr. Ford stated that he

---

[50] Carroll Kilpatrick, "Nixon Won't Flood Congress with New Legislation, Aides Say," *Washington Post,* Dec. 22, 1968, pp. Al and A6.
[51] James M. Haughton, "The Change in President: Plans Began Months Ago," *New York Time,* Aug. 26, 1974, p. 1.
[52] Morton Mintz and Stuart Auerbach, "Ford Solicits Suggestions on No. 2 Man," *Washington Post,* Aug. 11, 1974, p. Al.

had become President under sudden and difficult circumstances, without the usual time to plan a transition to power.[53]

FORD-CARTER TRANSITION

Before the 1976 election, the subject of Presidential transition was not publicly discussed by the Jimmy Carter campaign, reportedly because of what one Carter aide described as "the implied presumptuousness" of such considerations.[54] However, the actual planning for a Carter Administration began after the April 27, 1976 Pennsylvania primary, which Governor Carter considered the turning point in his achieving the Democratic nomination. According to press reports, while Jack Watson was still serving as Georgia finance chairman for the Carter campaign, he began drafting a detailed transition document with timetables and work-flow charts. The transition planning took place in Atlanta, Georgia, under the auspices of the "Carter-Mondale Policy Committee," in keeping with the low-profile approach said to be preferred by Governor Carter.[55]

Members of the Carter transition staff were lawyers, academicians, and government officials recruited by Jack Watson. The staff included: Harrison Wellford, a former congressional staff member; Larry Bailey, staff assistant to the U.S. Conference of Mayors; Sharleen Hirsch, an educational administrator; and Jules Sugarman, a public administrator. Staff members were assigned to task forces in the areas of community and human development, government organization, international security, economic policy, natural resources, and government regulation. The transition staff sought the advice of several persons with established expertise in transition planning, such as Clark Clifford, who worked on the Kennedy transition.[56]

On November 2, 1976, President Ford lost the election to Governor Carter, and the following day offered his "complete and whole-hearted support" in the transition to a new national leadership. President-elect Carter responded that he and Vice President-elect Mondale would take full advantage of this offer of close cooperation before Inauguration Day. Mr.

---

[53] Fred Austin, "Ford Begins Move to Reshape his Administration," *National Journal,* Dec. 14, 1974, val. 7, p.1877.
[54] Laurence Stern, "Transition Unit at Work for Carter," *Washington Post,* Aug. 9, 1976, p. Al.
[55] *Washington Post,* Aug. 9, 1976, p. A2.
[56] Ibid.

Ford designated presidential counselor John Marsh, Jr. as his transition liaison with Mr. Carter's transition representative, Jack Watson.[57]

On the day of his election, Mr. Carter received 50 transition papers with major policy initiatives pertaining to welfare reform, energy development and conservation, government reorganization, cabinet appointments, and budget reform.

A month after the election, Mr. Carter named his first cabinet nominees and directed his attention to the staffing of the approximately 200 top positions in his Administration.[58] He also announced that he would limit his time spent in Washington during the transition because he did not wish to act as if he were already President. Mr. Carter stated that Vice President-elect Mondale was in Washington and that "he is me as far as Washington is concerned."[59]

On November 22, 1976, President Ford and President-elect Carter met for an hour in the White House. The President-elect also met with the Director of the Office of Management and Budget (OMB), the Secretaries of Defense and Health, Education, and Welfare, and the Chairman of the Federal Reserve Board of Governors.

CARTER-REAGAN TRANSITION

As early as April 1980, Ronald Reagan began planning for a possible presidential transition when he met with a group of defense and foreign policy advisers before the Republican convention. The advisers were asked to prepare specific policy and budget recommendations for use in the first months of a Reagan Administration to enable him to begin work immediately after the inauguration. Coordinated by William Graham, an engineer with a California defense consulting firm, the experts included former Secretary of State Henry Kissinger, former President Ford, former White House chief of staff Alexander Haig, Senators John Tower and Richard Stone, Governor Bill Clements, former cabinet member Casper Weinberger, and former Ambassador Anne Armstrong.[60]

---

[57] Fredrick Smith, "Georgian Is Urged to Appoint 100 to Prepare Washington Takeover," *New York Times,* Nov. 4, 1976, p. 21.
[58] Jules Witcover, "Blueprint for Transition Going to Carter," *Washington Post,* Nov. 4, 1976, p. A18.
[59] Bruce F. Freed, "New Heads for Many Regulatory Bodies Expected to Be Named at Once by Carter," *Wall Street Jamal,* Nov. 11, 1976, p. 3.
[60] Lou Cannon, "Reagan Promises to Heal and Unify," *Washington Post,* Nov. 5, 1980, p. A20.

Following the Republican convention in July 1980, nearly 300 advisers were asked by Mr. Reagan to serve on 23 task forces to prepare reports due before Inauguration Day on economic and domestic issues.[61]

Ronald Reagan was elected the 40th President of the United States on November 4, 1980. President Carter pledged in his concession speech 'a very fine transition period, the best in history," and asked the country "to unite behind the President-elect.[62] On November 6, 1980, the President-elect named his formal transition team, a job he described as "translating campaign promises into reality." He named his campaign director, William Casey, to be chairperson of the transition executive committee, and campaign co-chairperson Anne Armstrong as vice chairperson. A personnel office was established under the leadership of E. Pendleton James to select people to fill approximately 2,700 top-level federal jobs.[63]

In November 1980, President-elect Reagan announced an executive branch transition organization consisting of five working groups responsible for the transfer of power. Under the direction of William Timmons, deputy director of transition, the working units coordinated transition efforts of various cabinet departments and other executive agencies. Bach cabinet department was assigned a specific team leader to oversee the transition. Mr. Reagan also named a 14-member Economic Policy Coordinating Committee that included many high-ranking officials from the Nixon and Ford Administrations.

President-elect Reagan said publicly that he did not intend to preempt the powers that belonged to President Carter until Inauguration Day 1981.[64] Mr. Carter's transition representative, Jack Watson, informed the Reagan group that the outgoing President intended to defer major policy decisions for the incoming Administration.[65] President-elect Reagan and his wife met with President Carter and his wife late in November 1980.

---

[61] Dick Kirschten, "The Reagan Team Comes to Washington, Ready to Get Off to a Running Start," *National Journal*, Nov. 15, 1980, p. 1926.
[62] Michael Getler, "Reagan Advisers Setting Up Special Teams to Oversee Transition," *Washington Post*, Nov.11, 1980, p. Al.
[63] Lee Lescaze, "Transition Team Is Announced," *Washington Post*, Nov. 7, 1980, p. Al.
[64] Lee Lescaze, "The Changing of the Guard Commences: Transition Team is Announced," *Washington Post*, Nov. 7, 1980, pp. Al, A3.
[65] T .R. Reid and Lee Lescaze, "Carter to Defer Action on Major Policy Issues," *Washington Post*, Nov. 13, 1980, p. Al.

REAGAN-BUSH TRANSITION

On November 8, 1988, George H. W. Bush became the 41st President, the first incumbent Vice President to be elected since Martin Van Buren in 1836. The following day, President-elect Bush announced the appointment of Craig Fuller, his former chief of staff, and Robert Teeter, his campaign strategist, as co-directors of the Bush transition effort. In addition, he named his longtime friend James Baker as an adviser on "key aspects" of the transition, and announced his intention to nominate Mr. Baker for Secretary of State. Mr. Bush stated that he wanted a "somewhat leaner" transition organization than was used in 1980. He also indicated that he would not seek to preempt President Reagan's authority during the transition period or "unduly influence decisions that are properly the President's."[66]

In mid-November 1988, President-elect Bush's transition office opened in Washington, D.C. Soon after, the Heritage Foundation delivered 2,500 resumes of persons recommended for jobs in the Bush Administration.[67] Mr. Bush proposed additional cabinet appointments on November 21, 1988, which included two from President Reagan's cabinet, Attorney General Richard Thornburgh and Education Secretary Lauro Cavazos.[68]

The smooth transition between the Reagan and Bush Administrations was further demonstrated on November 22, 1988, when White House Chief of Staff Kenneth Duberstein requested cabinet members and agency heads to provide information to the transition team on organizational matters, goals, and functions, resource descriptions, congressional oversight committees, regulatory programs, and other important issues relevant to each agency.[69] By the end of November 1988, most of the executive branch agencies had designated internal transition leaders to assist in an orderly transition with President-elect Bush's transition liaisons. Mr. Duberstein stated that the transition effort greatly benefited from the eight year partnership of President Reagan and President-elect Bush, and that "their philosophical compatibility cannot be underrated."[70]

---

[66] David Hoffman, "Bush Names Baker Secretary of State," *Washington Post,* Nov. 10, 1988, pp. Al and A38. -
[67] Judith Havemann, "Bush to Get 2,500 Conservative Resumes," *Washington Post,* Nov. 15, .1988, p. Al7.
[68] Jessica Lee, "Bush Taps Reagan Aides for Cabinet, Budget," *USA Today,* Nov. 22, 1988, p.8A
[69] Ibid.
[70] Jessica Lee, "Agencies Told to Give Data to Transition Team," *USA Today,* Nov. 23, 1988, p. 6A

BUSH-CLINTON TRANSITION

Following the August 1992 nomination of William Clinton at the Democratic National Convention, several of his closest aides began working on a transition document to prepare for a possible change of Administrations following the November election. Headed by Clinton campaign manager Mickey Kantor, the working group was known as the Clinton-Gore Pre-Transition Planning Foundation, and included former Mayor Henry Cisneros, attorney Warren Christopher, former Governor Madeleine Kunin, and attorney Vernon Jordan. Governor Clinton's pre-transition team was headquartered in Little Rock, Arkansas. The team collected information on past presidential transitions and prepared a series of transition briefing, books dealing with policy issues and proposed presidential agendas.[71]

In his concession speech following the election on November 3, 1992, President Bush stated that "our entire administration will work closely with his [Clinton's] team to ensure the smooth transition of power."[72] At a November 5 cabinet meeting, President Bush stated that his top aides would cooperate with the Clinton transition team:

> It's very important that we not be begrudging during the transition Let us all finish the job with the same class with which we served.[73]

It was later announced that Department of Transportation Secretary Andrew Card Jr. would head President Bush's transition team. In a radio address, President Bush stated that he would return to Texas after the inauguration, where he intended to retire from politics, and to "rededicate" himself to helping others.[74]

President-elect Clinton remained in Little Rock following the election, to lead transition reports and to meet with top advisers. His key transition appointments were not immediately announced, and press reports indicated that there was a dispute among his aides over who should lead the Clinton transition effort.[75] On November 6, 1992, it was announced that Vernon

---
[71] Adam Nagourney and Bill Nichols, "Clinton Camp Crafts Lineup," *USA Today,* Oct. 20, 1992, p. 2A. .
[72] George Bush, "The Way We See It...The People Have Spoken," *Washington Post,* Nov. 4, 1992, p. A22.
[73] Bill Nichols, "Bush Cooperation," *USA Today,* Nov. 6, 1992, p. 5A
[74] Thomas W. Lippmen, "Taking Full Responsibility for Loss," *Washington Post,* Nov. 8, 1992, p. Al.
[75] Adam Nagoumey and Bill Nichols, "Clinton Shifts Transition to High Gear," *USA Today,* Nov. 6, 1992, p. Al.

Jordan and Warren Christopher would head the Clinton transition team. It was also reported that Mr. Clinton would choose his cabinet officers in an orderly process, and that a "stringent set of ethics roles" would be used in the selection process.[76]

GENERAL CONSIDERATIONS

Each presidential transition is unique and brings with it the conditions and circumstances facing a particular President-elect that will help shape and influence his Administration. Despite the influence of unique circumstances, observers have identified a number of generally important transition issues based on past transition experiences.

Adequate Funding

Since enactment of the Presidential Transition Act of 1963, Presidents-elect have assembled extensive staffs and organizations to conduct their transitions. In the past, discussions of presidential transitions have often focused on the importance of adequate federal funding, culminating with the Reagan transition, when $1.25 million in private funds was raised by the Reagan Transition Foundation to meet additional transition expenses. Enactment of the Presidential Transitions Effectiveness Act in 1988 recognized this issue by increasing the total amount authorized for a presidential transition to $5 million. The legislation also authorized future transition funding to be increased by an inflation adjusted amount. For the 2000-2001 presidential transition, a total of $6.1 million has been appropriated for both the incoming and outgoing Administrations. An additional $1 million is available for GSA to implement its new transition responsibilities under the Presidential Transition Act of 2000.[77]

Pre-election Planning

The adequacy of federal funding, while a major consideration, is but one factor involved in determining the success of a presidential transition. A

---

[76] Ruth Marcus and Al Kamen, "Clinton Names Transition Chiefs," *Washington Post*, Nov. 7, 1992, p. A1.
[77] P.L. 106-426, Nov. 3, 2000.

review of the literature on presidential transitions indicates that another major concern pertains to time, or a lack of it, in completing everything that needs to be accomplished by a President-elect in the 11-week period between an election and an inauguration. A transition period that begins swiftly and smoothly can help to determine how successful a presidency will be. The expression "to hit the ground running" is frequently used to describe the goal of past transition teams to make their imprint quickly on a new presidential agenda.[78]

During its consideration of the Presidential Transition Effectiveness Act, the Senate Committee on Governmental Affairs reported that there was:

> ... near-unanimous agreement among past transition officials that a President-elect must undertake at least some advance planning during the general election campaign. A President-elect cannot wait until the morning after the election to start planning for the transition. In order for the President-elect to "hit the ground running," the candidate must lay the administrative groundwork before the campaign is over.[79]

Based on hearing testimony by representatives of the Harvard University Public/Private Careers Project, the committee found that such "pre-election transition planning may now be essential for ensuring post-election success."[80]

A decade later, the 106th Congress enacted the Presidential Transition Act of 2000, to authorize a formal orientation process between incoming political appointees and career federal employees. A July 18, 2000 report prepared by the Senate on Governmental Affairs Committee stated that "timely orientations to new appointees" were "virtually non-existent" during past transition periods. According to the committee, enactment of the new legislation was essential to avoid "missteps and outright errors made by newly appointed officials at executive branch agencies and in the White House."[81]

---

[78] James P. Pfiffner, *The Strategic Presidency: Hitting the Ground Running* (Chicago, Dorsey Press, 1988); pp. 9-18, see also: Robert K. Landers, "*The Dangers in Presidential Transitions"* (Washington: Editorial Research Reports, 1988), p. 1.
[79] V.S. Congress, Senate Committee on Governmental Affairs, *Presidential Transitions Effectiveness Act of 1988*, p. 6.
[80] Ibid., see also: *Presidential Transition Effectiveness Act,* hearings, 100th Cong., 1st and 2nd sess., Sept.17; Oct. 14, 1987, and Feb.17, 1988, (Washington: GPO, 1988), pp. 23-38.
[81] U.S. Congress, Senate Committee on Governmental Affairs, *Presidential Transition Act Of 2000*, 106th Cong., 2nd sess., S. Rapt. 106-348 (Washington: GPO, 2000), p. 2.

ORGANIZATIONAL DECISIONS

The day after the election, a President-elect and his staff normally must "shift gears" from winning the election to planning a successful transition. According to a 2000 Heritage Foundation project on the presidency, one of the most difficult tasks

Facing an incoming President is the merging of the campaign staffs and the newly- formed transition teams.[82] Elated by a winning campaign and a mandate for change by the electorate, a President-elect faces the transition period with great expectations. During the transition, the new Administration must act on campaign promises and quickly develop an administrative and legislative program. Author John Burke writes that the incoming Reagan Administration emphasized coordination between the transition team and the campaign staff to deflect the "rivalries and tensions" that had reportedly occurred during the previous transition of incoming President Carter.[83]

Crucial organizational decisions must be made as soon as possible on issues that will ultimately affect how well the new Administration succeeds. The President-elect and his staff must first make decisions related to key personnel appointments, and establish liaison with the representatives of the federal departments and agencies to ensure a smooth transition. Management and organizational issues should be resolved during the transition, so that substantive policy matters can be addressed on inauguration day.[84]

Incoming President George Bush, for example, had an obvious advantage during his well-organized 1988 transition, in that he was taking office as an incumbent Vice President. The day after his election, he immediately announced his transition team and several key staff appointments. His transition clearly benefited from the "good auspices" of former President Reagan because advice and information were "quickly conveyed, giving members of the transition both an easy start and a head start." In addition, President-elect Bush was able to select quickly his cabinet and executive appointees from many experienced executive branch officials.[85]

In a 1988 report on the Presidency and transitions, the National Academy of Public Administration stated that:

---

[82] Alvin S. Felzenberg, ed., The Keys to a Successful Presidency, p. 18.
[83] John P. Burke, Presidential Transitions: From Politics to Practice, p. 96.
[84] Carl Brauer, "Lost in Transition," *The Atlantic Monthly,* Nov.1988, p. 74.
[85] John P Burke, Presidential Transitions: From Politics to Practice, p. 225.

The initial decisions that a president makes when organizing the White House, determining its structure and functional responsibilities, and establishing patterns of interaction between it and other executive branch agencies will affect how these needs are met, and ultimately, how well a presidency works. Naturally, this will affect the achievement of policy objectives.[86]

CONTINUITY OF THE FEDERAL GOVERNMENT

A leadership void can occur during the transition period when the outgoing Administration has constitutional authority but diminished influence, and the President-elect has much influence but no authority. This is sometimes referred to as a "lame duck" Administration. A 1990 University of Virginia conference on presidential transitions found that, while the incumbent Administration was often intent on having a continued impact on public and foreign policy, "the mere existence of a president-elect and his developing Administration interferes with this effort."[87] A 1988 report by Editorial Research Reports discussed the "dangers associated with presidential transitions," both domestically and internationally, during the transition period. After the inauguration, difficult situations can also arise when a new and untested administration faces a sudden crisis or emergency.[88]

The day following his election, President-elect Clinton made a statement, asking foreign governments to continue recognizing President Bush as the "sole voice of U.S. policy." He also warned that "the greatest mistake any adversary could make would be to doubt America's resolve during this period of transition."[89]

Ideally, a President-elect who has been adequately briefed on policy issues by his transition teams during the weeks following the election will be better prepared to make crucial decisions upon entering office:

> Continuity of the federal government and responsiveness to the new political leadership are hallmark objectives of the traditional transition process. While incorporating these objectives, the extended transition process has been refuled to perform the functions of policy making,

---

[86] National Academy of Public Administration, *The Executive Presidency: Federal Management for the 1990s* (Washington: National Academy of Public Administration, 1988), p.5.
[87] Kenneth W. Thompson, ed., *Presidential Transitions: The Reagan to Rush Experience* (University of Virginia: University Press of America, 1993), p. 5.
[88] Landers, "Dangers of Presidential Transitions," *Editorial Research Reports,* pp. 528-529.
[89] Bill Nichols, "Clinton Sets New Sights," *USA Today,* Nov. 5, 1992, p. Al.

advice-giving and personnel selection simultaneously. The new administration must concentrate upon policy programs that are immediately relevant to show effectiveness on and immediately following January 20."[90]

SETTING PRIORITIES IN THE NEW ADMINISTRATION

A President-elect has 11 weeks to become informed in detail about the operations of the Federal Government before his Inauguration on January 20. The "mechanics" of managing a transition—the tasks, deadlines, and personnel decisions, budget and administrative procedures—generally occupy the initial phase of the transition process.[91]

However, the President-elect must also begin to focus on making substantive decisions on policy issues. Campaign promises are reviewed to form a policy agenda. Soon after taking office, the new President must prepare a legislative agenda to present to Congress.

The importance of the transition process cannot be underestimated in determining the ultimate success of an Administration. At least two authors advocate an "extended" transition that begins several months before the election and extends through at least the first session of Congress. If a President-elect has successfully focused on a "short list" of priorities or objectives that he wants to accomplish, he can dominate policymaking to achieve his goals during the honeymoon period that normally follows a election. By concentrating on a few key issues soon after taking office, many observers believe the President-elect can establish a public perception that he is in command of an aggressive policy agenda.

---

[90] Wallace Earl Walker and Michael R. Reopel, "Strategies for Governance: Transition and Domestic Policymaking fu the Reagan Administration," *Presidential Studies Quarterly,* val. 16, fall1986, p. 736.
[91] Walker and Reopel, "Strategies for Governance: Transition and Domestic Policymaking in the Reagan Administration," p. 739.

Part 2: Text of Presidential Transition Statutes

Chapter 3

PRESIDENTIAL TRANSITION ACT OF 2000: P.L. 106-293, OCTOBER 13, 2000

AN ACT

To provide for the training or orientation of individuals, during a Presidential transition, who the President intends to appoint to certain key positions, to provide for a study and report on improving the financial disclosure process for certain Presidential nominees, and for other purposes.

Be it enacted by the Senate and House of Representatives of the United States of America in Congress assembled,

Section 1. Short Title

This Act may be cited as the "Presidential Transition Act of 2000".

Sec. 2. Amendments to Presidential Transition Act of 1963.

Section 3(a) of the Presidential Transition Act of 1963 (3 U.S.C. 102 note) is amended—

(1) in the matter preceding paragraph (1) by striking including-- and inserting including the following:
(2) in each of paragraphs (1) through (6) by striking the semicolon at the end and inserting a period; and

(3) by adding at the end the following:

   (8) (A)(i) Not withstanding subsection (b), payment of expenses during the transition for briefings, workshops, or other activities to acquaint key prospective Presidential appointees with the types of problems and challenges that most typically confront new political appointees when they make the transition from campaign and other prior activities to assuming the responsibility for governance after inauguration.
   (ii) Activities under this paragraph may include interchange between such appointees and individuals who--
      (I) held similar leadership roles in prior administrations;
      (II) are department or agency experts from the Office of Management and Budget or an Office of Inspector General of a department or agency; or
      (III) are relevant staff from the General Accounting Office.
   (iii) Activities under this paragraph may include training or orientation in records management to comply with section 2203 of title 44, United States Code, including training on the separation of Presidential records and personal records to comply with subsection (b) of that section.
   (iv) Activities under this paragraph may include training or orientation in human resources management and performance-based management.
   (B) Activities under this paragraph shall be conducted primarily for individuals the President-elect intends to nominate as department heads or appoint to key positions in the Executive Office of the President.
   (9) (A) Notwithstanding subsection (b), development of a transition directory by the Administrator of General Services Administration, in consultation with the Archivist of the United States (head of the National Archives and Records Administration) for activities conducted under paragraph (8).
   (B) The transition directory shall be a compilation of Federal publications and materials with supplementary materials developed by the Administrator that provides information on the officers, organization, and statutory and administrative authorities, functions, duties, responsibilities, and mission of each department and agency.
   (10)(A) Notwithstanding subsection (b), consultation by the Administrator with any candidate for President or Vice President to

develop a systems architecture plan for the computer and communications systems of the candidate to coordinate a transition to Federal systems, if the candidate is elected.
(B) Consultations under this paragraph shall be conducted at the discretion of the Administrator.

Sec. 3. Report on Improving the Financial Disclosure Process for Presidential Nominees.

(a) In General- Not later than 6 months after the date of the enactment of this Act, the Office of Government Ethics shall conduct a study and submit a report on improvements to the financial disclosure process for Presidential nominees required to file reports under section 101(b) of the Ethics in Government Act of 1978 (5 U.S.C. App.) to the Committee on Governmental Affairs of the Senate and the Committee on Government Reform of the House of Representatives.
(b) Content of Report-
 (1) In general-The report under this section shall include recommendations and legislative proposals on
  (A) streamlining, standardizing, and coordinating the financial disclosure process and the requirements of financial disclosure reports under the Ethics in Government Act of 1978 (5 U.S.C. App.) for Presidential nominees;
  (B) avoiding duplication of effort and reducing the burden of filing with respect to financial disclosure of information to the White House Office, the Office of Government Ethics, and the Senate; and
  (C) any other relevant matter the Office of Government Ethics determines appropriate.
 (2) Limitation relating to conflicts of interest- The recommendations and proposals under this subsection shall not (if implemented) have the effect of lessening substantive compliance with any conflict of interest requirement.
(c) Authorization of Appropriations- There are authorized to be appropriated such sums as may be necessary to carryout this section.

Speaker of the House of Representatives.
Vice President of the United States and President of the Senate.

References

H.R 4931 (and S.2705), 106lh Congress
S. Rept 106-348, from the Committee on Governmental Affairs
7/24/2000: Referred to the House Committee on Government Reform.
7/31/2000: Referred to the Subcommittee on Government Management, Information and Technology;
9/13/2000: Committee on Government Reform discharged.
9/13/2000: Mr. Horn asked unanimous consent to discharge from committee and consider.
9/13/2000: Considered by unanimous consent.
9/13/2000: On passage Passed without objection.
9/13/2000: Motion to reconsider laid on the table. Agreed to without objection.
9/19/2000: Received in the Senate. Read twice. Placed on Senate Legislative Calendar under General Orders. Calendar No. 812.
9/28/2000: Passed Senate without amendment by Unanimous Consent.
9/28/2000: Cleared for White House.
9/29/2000: Message on Senate action sent to the House.
10/3/2000: Presented to President.
10/12/2000: Signed by President.
10/12/2000: Became Public Law No: 106-293.

Chapter 4

PRESIDENTIAL TRANSITIONS EFFECTIVENESS ACT: P.L. 100-398, AUGUST 17, 1988; 102 STAT. 985

AN ACT

To amend the Presidential Transition Act of 1963 to Provide for a more orderly transfer of executive power in connection with the expiration of the term of office of a President

Be it enacted by the Senate and House of Representatives of the United States of America in Congress assembled,

Section 1. Short Title

This Act may be cited as the "Presidential Transitions Effectiveness Act".

Sec 2. Presidential Transition Authorizations

(a) **AMENDMENT**- Section 5 of the Presidential Transition Act of 1963 (3U.S.C. 102 note) is amended-
  (1) by redesignating such section as section 6;
  (2) by inserting before such section the following heading:

Authorization of Appropriations

(3) by inserting "(a)" after the section designation;
(4) in paragraph (1), by striking out "$2,000,000" and inserting in lieu thereof "$3,500,000";
(5) in paragraph (2), by striking out "$1,000,000" and inserting in lieu thereof "$1,500,000"
(6) in paragraph (2), by inserting before the period at the end thereof the following: except that any amount appropriated pursuant to this paragraph in excess of $1,250,000 shall be returned to the general fund of the Treasury in the case where the former Vice President is the incumbent President; and
(7) by adding at the end thereof the following new subsection: "(b) The amounts authorized to be appropriated under subsection (a) shall be increased by an inflation adjusted amount, based on increases in the cost of transition services and expenses which have occurred in the years following the most recent Presidential transition, and shall be included in the proposed appropriation transmitted by the President under the last sentence of subsection (a)."

(b) **EFFECTIVE DATE**-The amendments made by subsection (a) of this section shall be effective upon enactment, except that the amendment made by paragraph (7) of such subsection shall take effect on October 1, 1989.

Sec. 3. Presidental Transition Financing And Personnel.

The Presidential Transition Act of 1963 (3 U.S.C. 102 note) is further amended by inserting after section 4 the following new section:

Disclosures of Financing and Personnel
Limitation on Acceptance of Donations

SEC. 5. (a)(l) The President-elect and Vice-President-elect (as a condition for receiving services under section 3 and for funds provided under section 6(a)(l)) shall disclose to the Administrator the date of contribution, source, amount, and expenditure thereof of all money, other than funds from the Federal Government, and including currency of the United

States and of any foreign nation, checks, money orders, or any other negotiable instruments payable on demand, received either before or after the date of the general elections for use in the preparation of the President-elect or Vice President-elect for the assumption of official duties as President or Vice President.

(2) The Preside elect and Vice-President-elect (as a condition for receiving such services and funds) shall make available to the Administrator and the Comptroller General all information concerning such contributions as the Administrator or Comptroller General may require for purposes of auditing both the public and private funding used in the activities authorized by this Act.

(3) Disclosures made under paragraph (1) shall be-
 (A) in the form of a report to the Administrator within 30 days after the inauguration of the President-elect as President and the Vice-President-elect as Vice President; and
 (B) made available to the public by the Administrator upon receipt by the Administrator.
  (b) (l) The President-elect and Vice-President-elect (as a condition for receiving services provided under section 3 and funds provided under section 6(a)(1)) shall make available to the public-
 (A) the names and most recent employment of all transition personnel (full-time or part-time, public or private, or volunteer) who are members of the President-elect or Vice-President elect's Federal department or agency transition teams; and
 (B) information regarding the sources of funding which support the transition activities of each transition team member.
(2) Disclosures under paragraph (1) shall be made public before the initial transition team contact with a Federal department or agency and shall be updated as necessary.
  (c) The President-elect and Vice-President-elect (as a condition for receiving services under section 3 and for funds provided under section 6(aX1)) shall not accept more than $5,000 from any person, organization, or other entity for purposes of carrying out activities authorized by this Act."

Sec. 4. Limitation on Expenditures of Certain Funds

(a) **USE OF AIRCRAFT** -Section 3(a)(4) of the Presidential Transition Act of 1963 (3 U.S.C. 102 note) is amended-
  (1) by inserting (A) after (4);
  (2) by adding at the end thereof the following new subparagraph:
  (B) When requested by the President-elect or Vice-President-elect or their designee, and approved by the President, Government aircraft may be provided for transition purposes on a reimbursable basis; when requested by the President-elect, the Vice-President-elect, or the designee of the president-elect or Vice-President-elect, aircraft may be chartered for transition purposes; and any collections from the Secret Service, press, or others occupying space on chartered aircraft shall be deposited to the credit of the appropriations made under section 6 of this Act;

(b) **DURATION OF EXPENDITURES**- Section 3(b) of the Presidential Transition Act of 1963 is amended to lead as follows:

(b) The Administrator may not expend funds for the provision of services and facilities under section 3 of this Act in connection with any obligations incurred by the President-elect or Vice-President-elect-
  (1) before the day following the date of the general elections held to determine the electors of President and Vice President under section 1 or 2 of title 3, United States Code; or
  (2) after 30 days after the date of the inauguration of the President-elect as President and the inauguration of the Vice President-elect as Vice President.

(c) **COMMENCEMENT OF EXPENDITURES**- Section 4 of the Presidential Transition Act of 1963 is amended by striking out "six months from the date of the expiration" and inserting "seven months from 30 days before the date of the expiration".

Sec 5. Disclosure of In-Kind Contributions to 1988-1989 Transition.

(a) **DISCLOSURE AS CONDITION OF RECEIPT OF FUNDS**- The President-elect and Vice-President-elect (as a condition for receiving services under section 3 and fur funds provided under

section 6(a)(1) of the Presidential Transition Act of 1963 (3 U.S.C. 102 note) shall provide an estimate to the Administrator of General Services of the aggregate value of in- kind contributions made during the period beginning on November 9, 1988, through January 20, 1989, received for transition activities for-
(1) transportation;
(2) hotel and other accommodations;
(3) suitable office space; and
(4) furniture, furnishings, office machines and equipment, and office supplies.
(b) **FORM AND AVILABILITY OF ESTIMATES**-The estimates made under subsection (a) shall be-
(1) in the form of a report to lhe Administrator of General Services within 90 days after January 20, 1989; and
(2) made available to the public by the Administrator upon receipt by the Administrator.

Sec 6. Travel and Transportation Expenses

Section 5723 of title 5, United States Code, is amended-

(1) in, subsection (a)(1), by striking out or (B) and inserting or (C);
(2) in subsection (a), by adding at the end thereof. "In the case of an appointee described in paragraph (1) who has performed transition activities under section 3 of the Presidential Transition Act of 1963 (3 U.S.C. 102 note), the provisions of paragraphs (1) and (2) may apply to travel and transportation expenses from the place of residence of such appointee (at the time of relocation following the most recent general elections held to determine the electors of the President) to the assigned duty station of such appointee"; and
(3) (3)in subsection (c), by adding at the end thereof the following: "In the case of an appointee described in subsection (a)(l) who has performed transition activities under section 3 of the Presidential Transition Act of1963 (3 U.S.C. 102 note), the travel or transportation shall take place at any time after the most recent general elections held to determine the electors of the President."

Sec. 7. Executive Agency Vacancies

(a) APPLICATION OF VACANCY PROVISIONS TO EXECUTIVE AGENCIES.-
  (1) Section 3345 of title 5, United States Code, is amended by striking out "Executive department" and inserting in lieu thereof "Executive agency (other than the General Accounting Office)".
  (2) The heading for section 3345 of title 5, United States Code, is amended to read as follows: "§3345. Details; to office of head of Executive agency or military department".
  (3) The table of section headings for chapter 33 of title 5, United States Code, is amended by amen ding the item relating to section 3345 to lead as follows: 3345. Details; to office of head of Executive agency or military department.
(b) EXTENSION OF TIME FOR INTERIM SERVICE.- Section 3348 of title 5, United States Code, is amended to lead as follows: §3348. Details; limited in time
  (a) A vacancy caused by death or resignation may be filled temporarily under section 3345, 3346, or 3347 of this title for not more than 120 days except that-
  (1) if a first or second nomination to fill such vacancy has been submitted to the Senate, the position may be filled temporarily under section 3345, 3346, or 3347 of this title (A) until the Senate confirms the nomination; or (B) until 120 days after the date on which either the Senate rejects the nomination or the nomination is withdrawn; or
  (2) if the vacancy occurs during an adjournment of the Congress sine die, the position may be filled temporarily until 120 days after the Congress next convenes, subject thereafter to the provisions of paragraph (1) of this subsection.
    (b) Any person filling a vacancy temporarily under section 3345, 3346, or 3347 of this title whose nomination to fill such vacancy has been submitted to the Senate may not serve after the end of the 120 day period referred to in paragraph (I)(B) or (2) of subsection (a) of this section, if the nomination of such person is rejected by the Senate or is withdrawn.

References

KR. 3932 (and S. 2037), 1001h Congress

H. Rept. 100-532, from the Committee on Government Operations

S. Rept. 100-317, from the Committee on Governmental Affairs

Mar. 16, 1988 - hearings held by Rouse Government Operations Subcommittee on Legislation and National Security.

Sept. 17, 1987, Oct. 14, 1987, and Feb. 17, 1988 -hearings held by Senate Committee on " Governmental Affairs

Mar. 31, 1988 -H.R. 3932 passed by the House

Apr; 26, 1988 -S. 2037 passed by the SenateApr.28, 1988 -RR. 3932 passed by the Senate, amended, in lieu of S. 2037

July. 26, 1988 -House concurred in Senate amendment, with an amendment

Aug. 2, 1988-Senate concurred in House amendment

Aug. 17, 1988-signed into law as P.L. 100-398

Chapter 5

PRESIDENTIAL TRANSITION ACT OF 1963, AMENDMENTS: P.L. 94-499, OCTOBER 14, 1976; 90 STAT. 2380

AN ACT

To revise the appropriation authorization for the Presidential Transition Act of 1963, and for other purposes.

Be it enacted by the Senate and House of Representatives, 8 of the United States of America in Congress assembled That (a) section 5 of the Presidential Transition Act of 1963 (3 U.S.C. 102 note) is amended to lead as follows:

"SEC. 5. There are hereby authorized to be appropriated to the Administrator such funds as may be necessary for carrying out the purposes of this Act, except that with respect to any one Presidential transition-
  (1) not more than $2,000,000 may be appropriated for the purposes of providing, services facilities to the President-elect and Vice President-elect under section 3, and
  (2) not more than $1,000,000 may be appropriated for the purposes of providing services and facilities to the former President and former Vice President under section 4.

The President shall include in the budget transmitted to Congress, for each year in which his regular term of office will expire, a proposed appropriation for carrying out the purposes of this Act."

(b) Section 3(a)(2) of the Presidential Transition Act of 1963 is amended by striking out "at rates not to exceed $100 per diem for individuals".

SEC. 2. Section (a)(2) of the Presidential Transition Act of 1963 is amended by striking out "or nonreimbursable".

SEC. 3. The amendment made by the first section of this Act shall take effect on-

    (1) the date of the enactment of this Act, or

    (2) October 1, 1976, whichever is later.

References

H.R. 14886, 94th Congress

H. Rept. 94-1442, from the Committee on Government Operations

S. Rept. 94-1322, from the Committee on Government Operations

Aug. 4, 1976-hearings held by House Government Operations Subcommittee on Legislation and National Security

Sept. 1, 1976-passed House

Sept. 30, 1976-passed Senate

Oct.14, 1976-signed into law as P.L. 94-499.

Chapter 6

PRESIDENTIAL TRANSITION ACT OF 1963: P.L. 88-277, MARCH 7, 1964; 78 STAT. 153

AN ACT

To promote the orderly transfer of the executive power in connection with the expiration of the term of office of a President and the inauguration of a new President.

Be it enacted by the Senate and House of Representatives of the United States of American in Congress assembled, That this Act may be cited as the Presidential Transition Act of 1963.

Purpose of this Act

SEC. 2. The Congress declares it to be the purpose of this Act to promote the orderly transfer of executive power in connection with the expiration of the term of office of a President and the inauguration of a new President. The national interest requires that such transitions in the office of President be accomplished so as to assure continuity in the faithful execution of the laws and in the conduct of the affairs of the Federal Government, both domestic and foreign. Any disruption occasioned by the transfer of the executive power could produce results detrimental to the safety and well-being of the United States and its people. Accordingly, it is the intent of the Congress that appropriate actions be authorized and taken to avoid or minimize any disruption. In addition to the specific provisions contained in this Act directed toward that purpose, it is the intent of the Congress that all officers of the Government so conduct the affairs of the Government for which they exercise responsibility and authority as (1) to be mindful of problems occasioned by transitions in the office of President, (2) to take appropriate lawful steps to avoid or minimize disruptions that might be occasioned by the transfer of the executive power, and (3) otherwise to promote orderly transitions in the office of President.

Services and Facilities Authorized to be Provided to Presidents- Elect and Vice-Presidents-Elect

SEC. 3. (a) The Administration of General Services, referred to hereafter in this Act as "the Administrator ," is authorized to provide, upon request, to each President-elect and each Vice- President, for in connection with his preparations for the assumption of official duties and President or Vice President necessary services and facilities, including-

(1) Suitable office space appropriately equipped with-furniture, furnishings, office machines and equipment, and office supplies, as determined by the Administrator, after consultation with the President-elect, the Vice-President-elect, or their designee provided for in subsection (e) of this section, at such place or places within the United States as the President-elect or Vice-President-elect shall designate;

(2) Payment of the compensation of members of office staffs designated by the President-elect or Vice-President-elect at rates determined by them not to exceed the rate provided by the Classification Act of 1949, as amended, for grade GS-18: *Provided,* That any employee of any agency of any branch of the Government may be detailed to such staffs on a reimbursable or nonreimbursable basis with the consent of the head of the agency; and while so detailed such employee shall be responsible only to the President-elect or Vice- President-elect for the performance of his duties: *Provided further,* That any employee so detailed shall continue to receive the compensation provided pursuant to law for his regular employment, and shall retain the fights and privileges of such employment without interruption. Notwithstanding any other law, persons receiving compensation as members of office

staffs under this subsection, other than those detailed from agencies, shall not be held or considered to be employees of the Federal Government except for purposes of Civil Service Retirement Act, the Federal Employees' Compensation Act, the Federal Employees' Group Life Insurance Act of 1954, and the Federal Employee Health Benefits Act of 1959;
(3) Payment of expenses for the procurement of services of experts or consultants or organizations thereof for the President-elect or Vice-President-elect, as authorized for the head of any department by section 15 of the Administrative Expenses Act of 1946, as amended (5 U.S.C. 55a), at rates not to exceed $100 per diem for individuals;
(4) Payment of travel expenses and subsistence allowances, including rental of Government or hired motor vehicles, found necessary by the President-elect or Vice- President-elect, as authorized for persons employed intermittently or for persons serving without compensation by section 5 of the Administrative Expenses Act of 1946; as amended (5 U.S.C. 73b-2), as may be appropriate;
(5) Communications services found necessary by the President-elect or Vice-President elect;
(6) Payment of expenses for necessary printing and binding, notwithstanding the Act of January 12, 1895, and the Act of March 1, 1919, as amended (44 U.S.C. 111);
(7) Reimbursement to the postal revenues in amounts equivalent to the postage that would otherwise be payable on mail matter referred to in subsection (d) of this section.
(b) The Administration shall expend no funds for the provision of services and facilities under this Act in connection with any obligations incurred by the President-elect or Vice President-elect before the day following the date of the general elections held to determine the electors of President and Vice President in accordance with title 3, United States Code, sections 1 and 2, or after the inauguration of the President-elect as President and the inauguration of the Vice-President-elect as Vice President.
(c) The terms "President-elect" and "Vice President-elect" as used in this Act shall mean such persons as are the apparent successful candidates for the office of President and Vice President, respectively, as ascertained by the Administrator following the general elections held to determine the electors of President and

Vice President in accordance with title 3, United States Code, sections 1 and 2.

(d) Each President-elect shall be entitled to conveyance within the United States and its territories and possessions of ail mail matter, including airmail, sent by him in connection with his preparations for the assumption of official duties as President, and such mail matter shall be transmitted as penalty mail as provided in title 39, United States Code, section 4152. Each Vice- President-elect shall be entitled to conveyance within the United States and its territories and possessions of ail mail matter, including airmail, sent by him under his written autograph signature in connection with his preparation for the assumption of official duties as Vice President.

(e) Each President-elect and Vice President-elect may designate to the Administrator an assistant authorized to make on his behalf such designations or findings of necessity as may be required in connection with the services and facilities to be provided under this Act. Not more than 10 per centum of the total expenditures under this Act for any President-elect or Vice-President-elect may be made upon the basis of a certificate by him or the assistant designated by him pursuant to this section by him or the assistant designated by him pursuant to this section that such expenditures are classified and are essential to the national security, and that they accord with the provisions of subsections (a), (b), and (d) of this section.

(f) In the case where the President-elect is the incumbent President or in the case where the Vice-President-elect is the incumbent Vice President, there shall be no expenditures of funds for the provision of services and facilities to such incumbent under this Act, and any funds appropriated for such purposes shall be returned to the general funds of the Treasury.

Services and Facilities Authorized to be Provided to Former Presidents and Former Vice Presidents

SEC. 4. The Administrator is authorized to provide, upon request, to each former President and each former Vice President, for a period not to exceed six months from the date of the expiration of his term of office as President or Vice President, for use in connection with winding up the affairs of his office, necessary services and facilities of the same general character as authorized by this Act to be provided to Presidents-elect and Vice Presidents-elect. Any person appointed or detailed to serve a former President or former Vice President under authority of this section shall be appointed or detailed in accordance with, and shall be subject to, an of the provisions of section 3 of this Act applicable to persons appointed or detailed under authority of that section. The provisions of the Act of August 25, 1958 (72 Stat. 838; 3 U.S.C. 102, note), other than subsections (a) and (e) shall not become effective with respect to a former President until six months after the expiration of his term of office as President.

Authorization of Appropriations

SEC. 5. There are hereby authorized to be appropriated to the Administrator such funds as may be necessary for carrying out the purposes of this Act but not to exceed $900,000 for any one Presidential transition, to remain available during the fiscal year in which the transition occurs and the next succeeding fiscal year. The President shall include in the budget transmitted to the Congress, for each fiscal year in which his regular term of office will expire, a proposed appropriation for carrying out the purposes of this Act.

References

H.R. 4638, 88th Congress
H. Rept. 88-301, from Committee on Government Operations
S. Rept. 88-448, from Committee on Government Operations
Conference Committee Report 88-1148
April 24, 1963 - hearings held by House Government Operations Subcommittee on Executive and Legislative Reorganization
July 25, 1963 - passed the House
Oct. 17, 1963 - passed the Senate, with amendments
Feb. 24, 1964 - Conference Report adopted and passed the Senate
Feb. 25, 1964 - Conference Report adopted and passed the House
Mar. 7, 1964 - signed into law as P.L. 88-277

INDEX

#

100th Congress, 10
106th Congress, 4, 13, 25
87th Congress, 6

A

Adams, President John, 3
Administration of General Services, 46
Administrative Expenses Act of 1946, 47
Administrator of General Services, 6, 32, 39
Arkansas, 23

B

Baker, James, 22
Buchen, Philip, 18
Bush Administration, 12, 22
Bush, President George H. W., 9, 22, 26

C

California, 20
Carter- Mondale Policy Committee, 19
Carter, President Jimmy, 9, 21, 26
Christopher, Warren, 23, 24
Civil Service Retirement Act, 47
Classification Act of 1949, 46
Clifford, Clark, 17, 19
Clinton Administration, vii, 13
Clinton, President William, 4, 12, 13, 23
Clinton-Gore Pre-Transition Planning Foundation, 23
Comptroller General, 37
Congress, 3, 4, 6, 7, 8, 10, 11, 12, 18, 25, 28, 31, 34, 35, 40, 41, 43, 44, 45, 49
Congressional Quarterly, 16, 17
Council for Excellence in Government, 14

D

Defense Department, 17
democracy, 3
Democratic National Committee, 5, 16

E

Editorial Research Reports, 25, 27
Eisenhower Administration, 17
Eisenhower, President Dwight D., 5
Eisenhower/Kennedy transition, 15
Ethics in Government Act of 1978, 33
executive power, 6, 35, 45

F

federal agencies, 7, 8, 9, 18
federal campaign funds, 11
Federal Election Commission (FEC), 10, 11, 12
Federal Employee Health Benefits Act of 1959, 47
federal employees, 14, 25
Federal Employees' Compensation Act, 47
Federal Employees' Group Life Insurance Act of 1954, 47
federal funding, 3, 4, 6, 10, 11, 24
federal funds, 4, 8, 10, 11, 13
Ford, President Gerald, 8
foreign policy, 16, 20, 27

G

General Accounting Office (GAO), 7, 8, 9, 10, 32, 40
General Services Administration (GSA), vii, 4, 8, 9, 11, 12, 13, 24
Georgia, 19
Gore Jr., Vice President Albert, 12

H

Haig, Alexander, 20
Harvard University Public/Private Careers Project, 25
Heritage Foundation, 3, 22, 26
Humphrey, Hubert, 7

I

Inauguration Day, vii, 15, 19, 21
inflation, 4, 24, 36
Internal Revenue Service, 10
international security, 19

J

Johnson, President, 7, 17
Jordan, Vernon, 23, 24
Justice Department, 8

K

Kennedy, President John F., 4, 5, 6, 15, 17
Kissinger, Henry, 20

L

Library of Congress, 12
Lincoln, Jr., Franklin, 17

M

Mondale, Vice President Walter, 9

N

National Academy of Public Administration, 26, 27
National Archives and Records Administration (NARA), 13, 32
national security, 48
New York, 18, 20
Nixon, President Richard M., 7, 17

O

Office of Government Ethics, 14, 33
Office of Management and Budget (OMB), 20, 32
Office of Personnel Management (OPM), 14
online web sites, 14
oversight committees, 22

Index

P

Pew Charitable Trusts, 14
political parties, 5, 6, 15
President-elect, 3, 4, 5, 6, 7, 8, 10, 11, 13, 14, 15, 16, 17, 19, 20, 21, 22, 23, 24, 25, 26, 27, 28, 32, 36, 37, 38, 43, 46, 47, 48
Presidential Transition Act (PTA), v, vi, vii, 3, 4, 6, 7, 8, 9, 10, 11, 12, 13, 14, 15, 17, 24, 25, 31, 35, 36, 38, 39, 43, 44, 45
Presidential Transition Act of 1963, v, vi, 3, 6, 15, 24, 31, 35, 36, 38, 39, 43, 44, 45
Presidential Transition Act of 2000, v, vi, vii, 4, 13, 14, 24, 25, 31
Presidential Transition Foundation, 10
Presidential Transitions Effectiveness Act, v, vi, 4, 10, 11, 12, 24, 25, 35
private funding, 37
private transition funds, 11
public funding, 11

Q

Quayle, Vice President Dan, 12

R

Reagan Administration, 20, 26, 28
Reagan Transition Foundation, 24
Reagan, President Ronald, 9, 12, 20, 21, 22, 26
records management, 32
Roosevelt, President Franklin D., 15

S

Scranton, William, 18
SEC. 3, 44, 46
SEC. 5, 36, 43, 49
Secret Service, 12, 38
selection process, 24
Senate Committee on Governmental Affairs, 10, 14, 25
Sorensen, Theodore, 16
Stevenson, Adlai, 16
Supplemental Appropriations Act of 1975, 8
Symington, Stuart, 16

T

Truman, President Harry, 15

U

United States, 21, 31, 32, 33, 35, 37, 38, 39, 40, 43, 45, 46, 47, 48

V

Van Buren, Martin, 22
Vice President-elect, 3, 4, 5, 6, 7, 8, 9, 11, 19, 20, 37, 38, 43, 47, 48

W

Washington, President George, 3
Watson, Jack, 19, 20, 21
Weinberger, Casper, 20
Whitehead, Clay, 18